PADDY THE ENGLISHMAN
PADDY THE IRISHMAN
AND
PADDY THE SCOTSMAN
JOKES

PADDY THE ENGLISHMAN
PADDY THE IRISHMAN
AND
PADDY THE SCOTSMAN
JOKES

DES MACHALE

MERCIER PRESS

MERCIER PRESS

Trade enquiries to CMD DISTRIBUTION,
55a Spruce Avenue, Stillorgan Industrial Park, Blackrock, Dublin

10 9 8

For
Conor, Rory and Ross MacHale

Printed in Ireland by Colour Books Ltd.

INTRODUCTION

What were the first jokes you ever heard as a child? If you grew up like me, then there is a good chance that they were the ones about Paddy the Englishman, Paddy the Irishman and Paddy the Scotsman. This book is a celebration of the three Paddies and only just in time too, because there will probably be a new EC law soon specifying that all these jokes must now be about Paddy the German, Paddy the Italian and Paddy the Belgian.

Over the years one gets to know very well the individual characteristics of the three Paddies as they appear in the jokes. Paddy the Englishman is a mere pawn, a veritable cipher, there just to introduce the scenario. Paddy the Scotsman is the canny one, careful with his financial expenditure and happy that he can put one over on Paddy the Englishman. He rarely realises that he in turn will be bettered by our Hibernian hero. Paddy the Irishman is nearly always the top dog in the story. He delivers the punch line with a crazy mixture of logic and insanity that leaves his opponents floundering in his wake.

Where did these three come from? Who knows? They are folk heroes, glorious reminders of an oral tradition of storytelling from the same stable as the king's three sons, the three wise men, the three bears, the Three Stooges and the Three Musketeers. They remind us of the Roman Triumvirate and maybe there is even a touch of the Holy Trinity about them.

There has always been something magical about the number three and my good friend Professor Christie Davies (alias Paddy the Welshman) explains these jokes diagramatically as follows: –

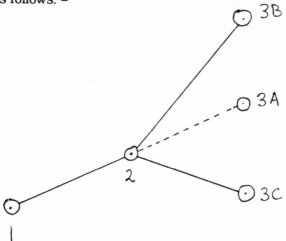

1 is Paddy the Englishman's position – he is merely a marker.

2 is Paddy the Scotsman's position, showing the trend or direction of the joke.

3A is Paddy the Irishman's expected position following the trend from Paddy the Englishman to Paddy the Scotsman. However, Paddy the Irishman is never to be found there. He is always at **3B** or **3C**, contrary to expectations.

Whatever the explanation of the three Paddies jokes, I'm sure all nations need jokes of this kind, if only to persuade themselves that they are as good if not better than their immediate neighbours.

Paddy the Englishman, Paddy the Irishman and Paddy the Scotsman got a job with a woman as furniture removal men. When she saw Paddy the Englishman and Paddy the Scotsman struggling to carry a wardrobe upstairs, she asked where Paddy the Irishman was.

'Oh he's in the wardrobe stopping the wire coat-hangers from rattling.'

Paddy the Englishman, Paddy the Irishman and Paddy the Scotsman were invited to a big party. Paddy the Englishman brought a flagon of cider. Paddy the Scotsman brought a bottle of whiskey. Paddy the Irishman brought his brother.

Paddy the Englishman and Paddy the Scotsman each had a horse but they couldn't tell them apart. So Paddy the Englishman cut the tail off his horse and all went well for a while, but then Paddy the Scotsman's horse lost his tail in an accident so they were back where they started. Finally, they consulted Paddy the Irishman and he said 'You two are a right pair of fools. Anyone can see that the black horse is three inches taller than the white horse.'

A very rich man died and left all his money to Paddy the Englishman, Paddy the Irishman and Paddy the Scotsman on condition that as he was being buried each of them would put £1,000 into his coffin in case he needed some money in the next world.

'Goodbye dear friend,' said Paddy the Englishman as he put £1,000 in notes into the
coffin.

'Goodbye generous friend,' said Paddy the
Scotsman as he put £1,000 in notes in too.

'So long, sucker,' said Paddy the Irishman
as he took out the £2,000 and put in a cheque
for £3,000.

Paddy the Englishman, Paddy the Irishman
and Paddy the Scotsman were playing Russian
roulette. Paddy the Englishman used a gun
with six chambers and no bullets; Paddy the
Scotsman used a gun with six chambers and
one bullet; Paddy the Irishman used a gun with
six chambers and six bullets – but he put the
gun to Paddy the Englishman's head.

Paddy the Englishman, Paddy the Irishman
and Paddy the Scotsman arrived at a railway
station in a state of inebriation just as the train
was about to leave. A helpful porter managed to
get Paddy the Englishman and Paddy the
Scotsman aboard as the train pulled out. Then
he turned to Paddy the Irishman and said, 'I'm
sorry sir that I couldn't get you aboard the
train.'

'My friends will be sorry too,' said Paddy the
Irishman, 'they just came to see me off.'

Paddy the Englishman, Paddy the Irishman
and Paddy the Scotsman all grew up in the
Gaeltacht and never learned to speak English.
One day they went to Dublin and Paddy the
Englishman heard a man saying, 'We three,' so

he went around all day saying, 'We three'.

Paddy the Scotsman heard a man saying 'For the want of money', so he went around all day saying, 'For the want of money'.

Paddy the Irishman heard a man saying 'We well deserve it', so he went around all day saying, 'We well deserve it'.

That evening as they were making their way home they came across a dead man lying on the ground. A policeman came up to them and said 'Who killed this man?'

'We three,' said Paddy the Englishman.

'Why did you do it?' asked the policeman.

'For the want of money,' said Paddy the Scotsman.

'You'll all go to jail,' said the policeman.

'We well deserve it,' said Paddy the Irishman.

Paddy the Englishman, Paddy the Irishman, Paddy the Scotsman, and Paddy the Welshman (making a guest appearance in this joke) were all flying together in an airliner. The captain announced that they were losing altitude rapidly and that one of them would have to jump out to save the others.

'I do this for the glory of Scotland,' said Paddy the Scotsman and he jumped out.

'We need to lose more weight,' said the captain, so Paddy the Welshman shouted ,'I do this for the glory of Wales', and jumped out.

'Sorry,' said the captain, 'I'm afraid we need to lose the weight of just one more person.'

'I do this for the glory of Ireland,' said Paddy the Irishman and threw out Paddy the Englishman.

Paddy the Englishman, Paddy the Irishman and Paddy the Scotsman were each allowed to ask God one question.

'When will England win the World Cup again?' asked Paddy the Englishman.

'Not for a hundred years,' said God, and Paddy the Englishman went away crying.

'When will Scotland gain independence?' asked Paddy the Scotsman.

'Not for two hundred years,' answered God, so Paddy the Scotsman went away crying.

'When will I get a bit of sense?' asked Paddy the Irishman, and God went away crying.

Paddy the Englishman, Paddy the Irishman and Paddy the Scotsman were stranded in a little boat together in the middle of the ocean. A little island appeared a short distance away so Paddy the Englishman walked across the water and returned with some food to eat. Then Paddy the Irishman walked across the water and returned with some coconut milk to drink. Not to be outdone, Paddy the Scotsman left the boat, started out for the island but disappeared from sight under the water.

'Do you think we should have told him where the stepping stones were?' asked Paddy the Englishman.

'What stepping stones?' asked Paddy the Irishman.

Paddy the Englishman, Paddy the Irishman and Paddy the Scotsman were invited to a fancy dress ball. They went as Alias, Smith and Jones.

Paddy the Englishman, Paddy the Irishman and Paddy the Scotsman each tendered for a big construction job paid for by government money.

'I'll do it for £2 million,' said Paddy the Englishman.

'How is that figure broken down?' asked the civil servant in charge of the scheme.

'£1 million for labour and £1 million for materials,' said Paddy the Englishman.

'I'll do it for £4 million,' said Paddy the Scotsman, 'that's £2 million for labour and £2 million for materials.'

'Look,' said Paddy the Irishman, 'my tender is for £6 million. That's £2 million for you, £2 million for me, and we'll give the other £2 million to Paddy the Englishman to do the job.'

Paddy the Englishman, Paddy the Irishman and Paddy the Scotsman took part in an international competition to see who had the greatest ability to endure foul smells. Each of them had to share a cage for as long as possible with an extremely smelly goat.

Paddy the Irishman lasted three minutes.

Paddy the Scotsman lasted four minutes.

Then Paddy the Englishman went in and after five minutes the goat came out.

Paddy the Englishman, Paddy the Irishman and Paddy the Scotsman were carpenters and were boasting about the high degree of accuracy they used in their work.

'I work to the nearest hundredth of an inch,' said Paddy the Englishman.

'I work to the nearest thousandth of an inch,' said Paddy the Scotsman.

'That wouldn't do me at all,' said Paddy the Irishman, 'I have to get it dead right.'

Paddy the Englishman, Paddy the Irishman and Paddy the Scotsman were appointed judges at the World Ice-skating Championships. The final competitor had a bit of a mishap. He slipped just as he was entering the rink, slid across the floor on his rear end, and demolished the judges' table with his feet.

'Could I have your marks gentlemen please, just for the record?' said the chief official.

'I award 0.0,' said Paddy the Englishman.

'I award 0.0,' said Paddy the Scotsman.

'I award 9.9,' said Paddy the Irishman.

'Hold on a moment,' said the chief official to Paddy the Irishman, 'how can you award such a high score for such a terrible performance?'

'Well,' said Paddy the Irishman, 'you've got to make allowances – it's as slippery as hell out there.'

Paddy the Englishman, Paddy the Irishman and Paddy the Scotsman were stranded on a little island in the middle of the Pacific Ocean and one day they found a magic lamp. When they rubbed it, a genie appeared and granted them each any one wish they desired.

'I'd like to be back in London,' said Paddy the Englishman and he was whisked back to London.

'I'd like to be back in Glasgow,' said Paddy the Scotsman and he too was whisked away.

'I'm very lonely here all on my own,' said Paddy the Irishman, 'I wish my friends were back again.'

Paddy the Englishman, Paddy the Irishman and Paddy the Scotsman had escaped from jail and were being followed by the police with tracker dogs. They decided to climb up into the trees to escape detection. As the dogs came sniffing at the base of the first tree, Paddy the Englishman, went 'miaow, miaow.'

'Come away,' said the policeman to the dogs, 'that's only a cat.'

'Chirp, chirp,' went Paddy the Scotsman.

'Come away,' said the policeman, 'that's only a bird.'

The dogs then began to sniff at the base of the tree where Paddy the Irishman was hiding.

'Moo, Moo,' went Paddy the Irishman.

Paddy the Englishman, Paddy the Irishman and Paddy the Scotsman were discussing sporting events.

'The closest race I ever saw,' said Paddy the Englishman, 'was a car race, in which one of the cars had been recently painted and won by the breadth of the coat of paint.'

'The closest race I ever saw,' said Paddy the Scotsman, 'was a horse race, in which a horse, stung by a bee, won by the length of the bee sting swelling on his nose.'

'The closest race I ever saw,' said Paddy the Irishman, 'is the Scotch.'

Paddy the Englishman, Paddy the Irishman

and Paddy the Scotsman were in charge of a hospital for the disabled and one day they were showing a millionaire around the place in the hope of getting a large donation from him.

Paddy the Englishman took him into a ward where there was a man with no arms.

'That's terrible,' said the millionaire, 'look here's a cheque for £50,000.'

Paddy the Scotsman took him into a ward where there was a man with no arms or legs.

That's terrible,' said the millionaire, 'look here's a cheque for £100,000.'

Paddy the Irishman took him into a ward where there was a bed with just a single tooth lying on the pillow.

'Oh my God,' gasped the millionaire, 'is that all that's left of the poor fellow?'

'Worse still,' said Paddy the Irishman, 'he's having that tooth out tomorrow.'

Paddy the Englishman, Paddy the Irishman and Paddy the Scotsman each put an odd number of spoons of sugar in his tea. Altogether, they put 16 spoons of sugar in their tea. How come?

Paddy the Englishman put in one spoon, Paddy the Scotsman put in one spoon and Paddy the Irishman put in 14 spoons which is a very odd number of spoons of sugar in a cup of tea.

Paddy the Englishman, Paddy the Irishman and Paddy the Scotsman attended the Olympic Games as spectators, but failed to get tickets for the main stadium.

Paddy the Englishman took a cannon-ball and got in by saying, 'I'm representing England in the shot.'

Paddy the Scotsman took a long pole and got in by saying, 'I'm representing Scotland in the pole vault.'

Paddy the Irishman took half a dozen stakes and three rolls of barbed wire and said to the official, 'I'm representing Ireland in fencing.'

Paddy the Englishman, Paddy the Irishman and Paddy the Scotsman were in court charged with stealing a horse, a donkey cart and a cow, respectively.

Paddy the Englishman said 'I've had that horse since he was a foal,' and his case was dismissed.

Paddy the Scotsman said 'I've had that cow since she was a calf,' and his case was dismissed.

Paddy the Irishman said, 'I've had that donkey cart since it was a wheelbarrow.'

A great fire was raging in Saudi Arabia and all the oil well fire experts in the world had failed to put it out. So they sent for Paddy the Englishman, Paddy the Irishman and Paddy the Scotsman. Our three heroes drove all the way out to Saudi Arabia in a little red van with Paddy the Irishman at the wheel. They put out the fire by driving the van right on top of the burning oil well and cutting off the supply of oxygen. Each of them was awarded a million dollars and they were asked what they would do with the money.

'I'm going to buy a golf course,' said Paddy the Englishman.

'I'm going to buy a distillery,' said Paddy the Scotsman.

'The first thing I'm going to do,' said Paddy the Irishman, 'is to have the brakes on that ould van fixed.'

Paddy the Englishman, Paddy the Irishman and Paddy the Scotsman were captured by the Devil. The Devil said he would send each of them to Hell unless they gave him a task he could not do.

Paddy the Englishman gave the Devil a block of ice and challenged him to turn it to steam. The Devil did this immediately so Paddy the Englishman was sent to Hell.

Paddy the Scotsman challenged the Devil to jump over Mount Everest. To his surprise the Devil did it with ease, so Paddy the Scotsman was sent to Hell.

Paddy the Irishman farted very loudly and said to the Devil, 'Catch that.'

Paddy the Englishman, Paddy the Irishman and Paddy the Scotsman were taking part in the final of a quiz.

Paddy the Englishman was asked, 'What year did the *Titanic* sink?' and he gave the correct answer.

Paddy the Scotsman was asked, 'How many people were on board the *Titanic*?' and he gave the correct answer.

Paddy the Irishman was asked, 'What were

their names and addresses?'

Paddy the Englishman, Paddy the Irishman and Paddy the Scotsman were all a bit the worse for drink and were travelling by train together.

'It's windy,' said Paddy the Englishman.

'No,' said Paddy the Scotsman, 'it's Thursday.'

'So am I,' said Paddy the Irishman, 'let's go and have a drink.'

Paddy the Englishman, Paddy the Irishman and Paddy the Scotsman were confessing their secret vices to each other.

'I'm a terrible gambler,' said Paddy the Englishman.

'I'm a terrible drinker,' said Paddy the Scotsman.

'My vice is much less serious,' said Paddy the Irishman, 'I just like to gossip about my friends.'

Paddy the Irishman played the following trick on Paddy the Englishman. He put his hand up against a brick wall and said, 'Now punch my hand as hard as you like.' When Paddy the Englishman attempted to do so, Paddy the Irishman pulled his hand away and so Paddy the Englishman banged his fist against the wall.

After a good laugh all round, Paddy the Englishman went away to try out the trick on Paddy the Scotsman.

'We really would need a brick wall to do this

trick properly,' he told him, 'but there doesn't seem to be one around. Never mind, I'll put my hand in front of my face.'

Paddy the Englishman, Paddy the Irishman and Paddy the Scotsman applied for a vacancy with the phone company so the foreman said 'I'll give you all a trial day to see how many telegraph poles you can lay in that time.' At the end of the day Paddy the Englishman had done twenty-seven poles and Paddy the Scotsman had laid twenty-four.

'How many did you manage?' the foreman asked Paddy the Irishman.

'Five,' answered Paddy the Irishman.

'Well,' said the foreman, 'your friends managed over fifty between them.'

'Yes,' said Paddy the Irishman, 'but look how much they left sticking out of the ground.'

Paddy the Englishman, Paddy the Irishman and Paddy the Scotsman joined a silent order of monks who had porridge for breakfast every morning. If a monk was really desperate to say something every three years he was allowed to speak one sentence, so after three years Paddy the Englishman applied for permission to speak. This was granted and he said with great passion and feeling 'I HATE PORRIDGE!'

After three more years Paddy the Scotsman applied for permission to speak and this request too was granted.

'I HATE PORRIDGE!' shouted Paddy the Scotsman.

After three more years, Paddy the Irishman applied for permission to speak and after much deliberation his request was granted.

'I'm leaving,' said Paddy the Irishman. 'I can't stand this non-stop complaining about porridge.'

Paddy the Englishman, Paddy the Irishman and Paddy the Scotsman went to confessions and each had to say a prayer for his penance. Paddy the Englishman was told to say the Our Father, so he began, 'Our Father, which art in Heaven ...'

Paddy the Scotsman was told to say the Hail Mary, so he began 'Hail Mary, full of grace ....'

Paddy the Irishman was told to say the Angelus, so he began 'Boing, boing, boing ...'

Paddy the Englishman, Paddy the Irishman and Paddy the Scotsman were discussing what was the world's greatest invention.

Paddy the Englishman said it was money because it made world trade possible.

Paddy the Scotsman said it was the motor car because it made travel so easy.

Paddy the Irishman said it was venetian blinds because if it wasn't for venetian blinds it would be curtains for all of us.

Paddy the Englishman, Paddy the Irishman and Paddy the Scotsman applied for a job as chauffeur to a rich lady.

'I'm such a good driver,' said Paddy the Englishman, 'I can go within six inches of a cliff edge without driving over.'

'I can go within an inch of the edge of a cliff without driving over,' said Paddy the Scotsman.

'And how close to the cliff edge can you drive?' the lady asked Paddy the Irishman.

'I keep as far away from cliffs with the car as I possibly can,' said Paddy the Irishman.

Paddy the Englishman, Paddy the Irishman and Paddy the Scotsman were up in court charged with playing an illegal card game for money.

'I wasn't gambling in an illegal card game your honour,' said Paddy the Englishman to the judge, 'I was just showing my friends a magic trick with the cards.'

'Case dismissed,' said the judge.

'I wasn't gambling at cards either your honour,' said Paddy the Scotsman, 'I was just trying to calculate the odds of getting a full house.'

'Case dismissed also,' said the judge.

'Now,' he said to Paddy the Irishman, 'were you playing an illegal card game?'

'Who with?' said Paddy the Irishman.

Paddy the Englishman, Paddy the Irishman and Paddy the Scotsman set up a furniture removal company. One day they spent over two hours trying to move a wardrobe which was wedged in a narrow stairway.

'It's no use,' said Paddy the Englishman to Paddy the Scotsman, 'we'll never get it upstairs,'

'Upstairs?' said Paddy the Irishman, 'I

thought we were trying to get it downstairs.'

Paddy the Englishman, Paddy the Irishman and Paddy the Scotsman bought a bottle of good whiskey and marked the bottle into three clear portions – the one on the top for Paddy the Englishman, the one in the middle for Paddy the Scotsman and the one on the bottom for Paddy the Irishman. They decided to go to bed and drink the whiskey the next day.

However, when they got up the next morning, Paddy the Englishman and Paddy the Scotsman were dismayed to find that the whiskey was all gone. So they woke Paddy the Irishman from his drunken slumbers and asked him to explain.

'I felt like a drink during the night,' said Paddy the Irishman, 'so I got up and opened the bottle of whiskey, but I had to drink through your two portions to get to my own.'

Paddy the Englishman, Paddy the Irishman and Paddy the Scotsman were asked in a survey what nationality they would like to have been born if they hadn't been born the nationality they were.

'If I hadn't been born English,' said Paddy the Englishman, 'I would have liked to have been French.'

'If I hadn't been born Scottish,' said Paddy the Scotsman, 'I would have liked to have been Irish.'

'If I hadn't been born Irish,' said Paddy the Irishman, 'I would have been ashamed of myself.'

Paddy the Englishman, Paddy the Irishman and Paddy the Scotsman were taking an intelligence test. They were all asked the question: 'Which bird does not build its own nest?'

'It's the canary,' said Paddy the Englishman. 'He lives in a cage.'

'It's the parrot,' said Paddy the Scotsman. 'He lives in the zoo.'

'It's the cuckoo,' said Paddy the Irishman.

'Very good,' said the examiner, 'how did you know that?'

'Everybody knows the cuckoo lives in a clock,' said Paddy the Irishman.

Paddy the Englishman, Paddy the Irishman and Paddy the Scotsman became policemen and were sent out on patrol together. This was because Paddy the Englishman could read, Paddy the Scotsman could write and Paddy the Irishman was a Special Branch man to keep an eye on two such dangerous intellectuals.

Paddy the Englishman, Paddy the Irishman and Paddy the Scotsman were trying to cross a shark-infested river in the jungle. Paddy the Englishman was first to cross and he lost an arm to a shark.

Next Paddy the Scotsman crossed and he lost a leg.

Finally, Paddy the Irishman waded across the river without a shark laying a tooth on him.

'How did you manage that?' they asked him.

'It was easy,' smiled Paddy the Irishman, 'I just wore a tee-shirt with *England for the World Cup* on it. Not even sharks would swallow that.'

Paddy the Englishman, Paddy the Irishman and Paddy the Scotsman were all seriously ill in hospital. Paddy the Scotsman asked if he could hear the bagpipes for one last time before he died and his request was granted. Paddy the Scotsman recovered but every other patient in the hospital died.

Paddy the Englishman, Paddy the Irishman and Paddy the Scotsman were reading a newspaper article about which nationalities' brains were for sale for transplant purposes. An Irishman's or a Scotsman's brain could be bought for £500 but an Englishman's brain cost £10,000.

'That proves,' said Paddy the Englishman, 'that Englishmen are much cleverer than Irishmen or Scotsmen.'

'No it doesn't,' said Paddy the Irishman, 'it just means that an Englishman's brain has never been used.'

Paddy the Englishman, Paddy the Irishman and Paddy the Scotsman met the world's foremost wine expert who could, blindfold, tell the name and origin of any sample of wine. Paddy the Englishman handed him a sample and after a few tastes the expert said, 'That's a claret, French 1953 I would say.'

'Correct,' said an impressed Paddy the Englishman.

Paddy the Scotsman handed him a sample and after a few minutes the expert said 'That's a Chianti, Italian, 1979.'

'Correct,' said Paddy the Scotsman.

Paddy the Irishman piddled into a glass and handed it to the blindfold expert. After a few tastes, he spluttered and said, 'Why that's urine.'

'Correct,' said Paddy the Irishman, 'but whose?'

Paddy the Englishman, Paddy the Irishman and Paddy the Scotsman went into a bar and Paddy the Irishman said, 'Look at the size of that hump on the barman's back.'

'Be careful,' said Paddy the Scotsman, 'that's Paddy the Englishman's brother.'

'Oh really?' said Paddy the Irishman, 'I was just going to say how nice it looked on him.'

Paddy the Englishman, Paddy the Irishman and Paddy the Scotsman were each boasting that they had the best job in the world.

'I work in the Royal Mint,' said Paddy the Englishman, 'and I can take home as much money as I want.'

'I'm the chief taster in a whiskey distillery,' said Paddy the Scotsman, 'and the free samples are out of this world.'

'But I've got the best job of all,' said Paddy the Irishman, 'I'm working in a British crematorium, burning Englishmen and Scotsmen and getting paid for it.'

Paddy the Englishman, Paddy the Irishman and Paddy the Scotsman were travelling by jumbo jet. The captain got worried that they were going to crash so he asked all the passengers to do something religious.

Paddy the Englishman sang 'Nearer my God to thee'.

Paddy the Scotsman recited 'The Lord's prayer'.

Paddy the Irishman took his cap off and went around and took up a collection.

Paddy the Irishman was showing Paddy the Englishman and Paddy the Scotsman the biggest building in his native town.

Paddy the Scotsman said, 'Back home we have buildings ten times the size of that.'

Paddy the Englishman said, 'Back home we have buildings a hundred times the size of that.'

'I'm not surprised,' said Paddy the Irishman. That's the local lunatic asylum.'

Paddy the Englishman was telling Paddy the Irishman and Paddy the Scotsman about his travels and adventures in India.

'I once saw a man,' he told them, 'being beheaded with his hands tied behind his back, and do you know what happened? He picked up his head and put it back on his shoulders again.'

'How could he do that,' asked Paddy the Scotsman, 'when his hands were tied behind his back?'

'You fool,' said Paddy the Irishman, 'couldn't he pick it up with his teeth.'

Paddy the Englishman, Paddy the Irishman and Paddy the Scotsman were spending the night in a haunted house. At about 1 am Paddy the Englishman woke up and saw a ghost which said, 'I am the ghost with one black eye', so Paddy the Englishman ran screaming from the building. At about 2 am Paddy the Scotsman woke up and heard the ghost saying, 'I am the ghost with one black eye', so he too ran screaming from the building. At 3 am Paddy the Irishman woke up and heard the ghost saying, 'I am the ghost with one black eye'.

Paddy the Irishman said, 'If you don't shut up you'll be the ghost with two black eyes.'
(Told to me by a nine year old)

Paddy the Englishman, Paddy the Irishman and Paddy the Scotsman spent the night in a haunted house. In their bedroom was a table and on the table was a twenty pound note.

At 1 am Paddy the Englishman woke up and tried to take the note but a voice rang out, 'I am the ghost of Auntie Mabel, that twenty pounds stays on the table.'

At 2 am Paddy the Scotsman woke up and tried to take the note but again a voice rang out, 'I am the ghost of Auntie Mabel, that twenty pounds stays on the table.'

At 3 am Paddy the Irishman woke up and as he reached for the money once again the voice rang out, 'I am the ghost of Auntie Mabel, that twenty pounds stays on the table.'

Paddy the Irishman sang out, 'I am the ghost of Davy Crockett, that twenty pounds goes in my pocket.' *(Told to me by a seven year old)*

Paddy the Englishman, Paddy the Irishman and Paddy the Scotsman were captured by the Devil and would be sent to Hell if they could not give him an impossible task to do. 'Touch the moon,' said Paddy the Englishman. The Devil did and Paddy the Englishman was sent to Hell. '

'Darken the sun,' said Paddy the Scotsman. The Devil did and Paddy the Scotsman was sent to Hell.

Paddy the Irishman thought for a moment, cleared his throat and spat on the ground. 'Swim in that,' he said to the Devil.

Paddy the Englishman, Paddy the Irishman and Paddy the Scotsman were spending the night in a haunted house.

At about 1 am Paddy the Englishman woke up and heard a spooky voice saying, 'when I get ya, I'm going to eat ya', so he ran in terror from the house.

At about 2 am Paddy the Scotsman woke up and heard a spooky voice saying ,'when I get ya, I'm going to eat ya', so he too ran in terror from the house.

At about 3 am Paddy the Irishman woke up and heard the same spooky voice saying, 'when I get ya, I'm going to eat ya', so he decided to investigate. He crept upstairs, opened a door, and there was a fellow picking his nose and saying, 'when I get ya, I'm going to eat ya'.

Paddy the Englishman, Paddy the Irishman and Paddy the Scotsman got jobs as lumberjacks and each was given an electric power saw. On their first day at work Paddy the Englishman cut down a hundred trees, Paddy the Scotsman cut down eighty trees but Paddy the Irishman could manage only sixty trees. The boss was surprised that Paddy the Irishman was so far behind the others, so he said to him, 'Give me a look at your saw to see if it's O.K.' So he switched it on and it went 'brmm, brmm.'

'What's that noise?' said Paddy the Irishman.

Paddy the Englishman, Paddy the Irishman and Paddy the Scotsman were living in digs together. One night Paddy the Englishman and Paddy the Scotsman decided to play a trick on Paddy the Irishman. When he was asleep they shaved off his fine head of hair and left him as bald as an egg. Rushing out to work next morning he happened to glance in the mirror. 'Crikey,' he said, 'the landlady has called the wrong man for work.'

Paddy the Englishman, Paddy the Irishman and Paddy the Scotsman went into a pub. Paddy the Englishman stood a round. Paddy the Irishman stood a round. Paddy the Scotsman stood around.

Paddy the Englishman, Paddy the Irishman and Paddy the Scotsman were passengers on board the cross channel ferry when Paddy the Englishman fell into the sea.

Paddy the Scotsman shouted, 'man over-board, throw in a buoy', so Paddy the Irishman grabbed a little lad of eight and threw him over-board.

Paddy the Scotsman shouted, 'Not that sort of boy. I meant a cork buoy.'

'How the hell am I supposed to know what part of Ireland he comes from?' said Paddy the Irishman.

Paddy the Englishman, Paddy the Irishman and Paddy the Scotsman were discussing how and at what age they would like to die. 'I'd like to die at the age of eighty,' said Paddy the Englishman, 'from an overdose of Yorkshire pudding.'

'I'd like to die at the age of ninety,' said Paddy the Scotsman, 'drowned in a vat of Scotch whisky.'

'I'd like to die at the age of a hundred,' said Paddy the Irishman, 'shot by a jealous husband.'

Paddy the Englishman, Paddy the Irishman and Paddy the Scotsman were accosted by a mugger. Paddy the Englishman handed over his money but Paddy the Irishman said to Paddy the Scotsman 'here's that £100 I owe you'.

Paddy the Englishman, Paddy the Irishman and Paddy the Scotsman were being inter-viewed by a census official who asked for their profession and place of residence.

Paddy the Englishman answered that he

was unemployed and of no fixed abode. Paddy the Scotsman answered that he too was unemployed and of no fixed abode. Paddy the Irishman answered that he helped Paddy the Englishman and Paddy the Scotsman and lived in the flat above them.

Paddy the Englishman, Paddy the Irishman and Paddy the Scotsman were applying for a job as a lumberjack so the foreman gave each of them an axe and told then to cut down trees for a day. Paddy the Englishman cut down a hundred trees while Paddy the Scotsman cut down two hundred, but Paddy the Irishman cut down five hundred trees so he got the job.

'That's terrific,' said the foreman. 'Tell me, where did you learn to cut down trees like that?'

'In the Sahara Desert,' said Paddy the Irishman.

'But there aren't any trees in the Sahara Desert,' said the foreman.

'Not now there aren't,' said Paddy the Irishman.

Paddy the Englishman, Paddy the Irishman and Paddy the Scotsman were marooned on a little desert island and were wondering how to escape.

'Let's build a raft,' said Paddy the Englishman.

'No, let's build a boat,' said Paddy the Scotsman.

'No need to, we're saved,' said Paddy the Irishman. 'Here comes the *Titanic*.'

Paddy the Englishman, Paddy the Irishman and Paddy the Scotsman were watching a train coming in to a station.

'Here it comes,' said Paddy the Englishman.

'Here she comes,' said Paddy the Scotsman.

'Here he comes,' said Paddy the Irishman.

Who was right?

Paddy the Irishman because it was a mail train.

Paddy the Englishman, Paddy the Irishman and Paddy the Scotsman were captured by pirates and were each condemned to forty lashes. However, as a concession, each was allowed to have something on his back.

'Just rub a little palm oil on my back,' said Paddy the Englishman, 'and I'll take the forty lashes like a man.'

'Just rub some Scotch whisky on my back,' said Paddy the Scotsman, 'and I won't feel a thing.'

Said Paddy the Irishman. 'Just put Paddy the Englishman and Paddy the Scotsman across my back and I'll take the forty lashes like a man and I won't feel a thing either.'

Paddy the Englishman, Paddy the Irishman and Paddy the Scotsman were all staying in digs together.

One day one of the landlady's chickens died so they all had roast chicken for dinner.

The next day the landlady's pig died so they all had roast pork chops for dinner.

On the third day the landlady's husband died, so they all left.

Paddy the Englishman, Paddy the Irishman and Paddy the Scotsman all went to the pub together.

Paddy the Englishman spent £30, Paddy the Irishman spent £50 and Paddy the Scotsman spent a very pleasant evening indeed.

Paddy the Englishman, Paddy the Irishman and Paddy the Scotsman were playing poker together but Paddy the Irishman had no luck at all. He lost game after game after game until his money was nearly all gone. Then finally in the small hours of the morning he couldn't believe his eyes when he saw that he had drawn four aces. As the stakes rose higher and higher the tension became too much for Paddy the Scotsman who lurched forward across the table – dead.

'What will we do?' said Paddy the Englishman.

'Out of respect for the dead,' said Paddy the Irishman, 'I propose that we play this hand standing up.'

Paddy the Englishman, Paddy the Irishman and Paddy the Scotsman went into a restaurant which advertised that they would pay £1,000 if you ordered a dish they could not serve.

'I'll have yak's eye soup,' said Paddy the Englishman but to his amazement he was served with a steaming hot bowl of yak's eye soup.

'I'll have cuckoo's nest soup,' said Paddy the Scotsman and he was amazed to have his order served, beautifully garnished.

'I'll have elephant's kidneys on toast,' said

Paddy the Irishman, and a few minutes later the waiter returned with a cheque for £1,000.

'I knew you'd never have elephant's kidneys,' said Paddy the Irishman.

'We have lots of them,' said the waiter, 'but we've just run out of bread.'

Paddy the Englishman and Paddy the Scotsman were abroad so they phoned Interpol and sent a gorgeous parrot to their friend Paddy the Irishman.

When they arrived home however Paddy the Irishman opened the oven and produced the parrot well and truly roasted saying, 'Let's have some lovely roast duck for dinner.'

'That isn't a duck you fool,' they said to him. 'It's a parrot and it could speak seven different languages.'

'In that case,' said Paddy the Irishman, 'why didn't it say something before I put it in the oven?'

Paddy the Englishman, Paddy the Irishman and Paddy the Scotsman went into a sweet shop together.

'I'll have 20p worth of those sweets up there,' said Paddy the Englishman, pointing to a jar on a high shelf.

So the shopkeeper got out his ladder, climbed up, took down the jar of sweets and gave Paddy the Englishman 20p worth, climbed the ladder, and put the jar back up again.

'Now what do you want?' he asked Paddy the Scotsman.

'I want 20p worth of those sweets also,' said

Paddy the Scotsman, so the shopkeeper again got out his ladder, climbed up, gave Paddy the Scotsman his 20p worth and was just about to climb back up again when he said to Paddy the Irishman, 'I suppose you want 20p worth of those sweets too?'

'No,' said Paddy the Irishman.

So the shopkeeper climbed up the ladder, put the jar away, climbed down the ladder, and put the ladder away.

'Now,' he said to Paddy the Irishman, 'what do you want?'

'10p worth of those sweets,' said Paddy the Irishman.

These were the last words of our three heroes.

Paddy the Englishman: Thank God I die in England.

Paddy the Scotsman: Thank God I don't die in England.

Paddy the Irishman: How can they make any profit on this stuff at £2 a bottle?

Paddy the Englishman, Paddy the Irishman and Paddy the Scotsman all claimed to be the most famous of the three of them.

'I'm known all over England,' said Paddy the Englishman.

'I'm known all over the world and other places besides,' said Paddy the Scotsman.

'Let me show you both how famous I am,' said Paddy the Irishman. So they all travelled to Italy together, to the Vatican and into St Peter's Square. Paddy the Englishman and Paddy the Scotsman looked up and saw Paddy the Irishman standing on the balcony with his arm around the Pope, waving to the crowd. An Italian standing nearby said to Paddy the Englishman and Paddy the Scotsman, 'Who's that fellow on the balcony beside Paddy the Irishman?'

Paddy the Englishman, Paddy the Irishman and Paddy the Scotsman were forced by a wicked witch to jump over a cliff but their fairy godmother obtained for them a concession that whatever word they spoke before they jumped they would land in.

'Feathers,' said Paddy the Englishman, and he landed on a nice soft bed of feathers.

'Cushions,' said Paddy the Scotsman, and he landed on a nice big soft cushion.

Paddy the Irishman ran up to the edge of the cliff, tripped, and, as he fell over he said, 'Oh poos.' *(Told to me by my 9 year old son and he didn't say 'poos' either!)*

Paddy the Englishman, Paddy the Irishman and Paddy the Scotsman went into a shop during the war.

'I'll have an apple,' said Paddy the Englishman.

'That'll be £2,' said the shopkeeper. 'The price is gone up with the war.'

'I'll have an orange,' said Paddy the Scotsman.

'That'll be £3,' said the shopkeeper. 'The price is gone up with the war.'

Then he noticed that Paddy the Irishman had a hump on his back.

'What's that on your back?' he asked him.

'It's me bum,' said Paddy the Irishman. 'It's gone up with the war.'

Paddy the Irishman had just graduated from night school and was answering technical questions put to him by Paddy the Englishman and Paddy the Scotsman.

'How does the telephone work?' Paddy the Englishman asked Paddy the Irishman.

'The telephone,' said Paddy the Irishman, 'is like a big dog with his tail in Dublin and his head in London. When you step on his tail in Dublin, he barks in London.'

'That's a pretty good explanation,' said Paddy the Scotsman. 'Now tell me, how does the radio work?'

'The radio,' said Paddy the Irishman, 'is exactly the same as the telephone, but without the dog.'

Paddy the Englishman, Paddy the Irishman and Paddy the Scotsman were in a pub one night when a politician came in looking for votes.

'I'll buy a pint of stout,' said the politician 'for whichever of the three of you gives me the best reason for voting for the government.'

'I'll vote for your government,' said Paddy the Englishman, 'because it is my democratic duty to do so.'

'I'll vote for your government,' said Paddy the Scotsman, 'because I hate the opposition.'

'I'll vote for your government,' said Paddy the Irishman, 'because I want that pint.'

Paddy the Englishman, Paddy the Irishman and Paddy the Scotsman were being interviewed for a job as head of the Government Information Services. Each was asked the question 'What is two plus two?'

Paddy the Englishman answered 'four'. He didn't get the job because the interview board felt he was too blunt and tactless.

Paddy the Scotsman answered 'usually four'. He didn't get the job because the interview board felt he was too indecisive.

It was Paddy the Irishman who got the job. He said to the board 'What would you like the answer to be?'

Paddy the Englishman, Paddy the Irishman and Paddy the Scotsman were in a noisy pub one evening.

'Will you lend me £10?' Paddy the Scotsman shouted to Paddy the Irishman.

'You'll have to speak up a bit,' said Paddy the Irishman, 'I can't hear a word you're saying with all the noise in here.'

'Will you lend me £10?' screamed Paddy the Scotsman at the top of his voice.

'It's no use,' said Paddy the Irishman, 'I still cannot hear a word you're saying.'

'Look,' said Paddy the Englishman,' standing beside them, 'I can hear him quite clearly.'

'In that case,' said Paddy the Irishman, 'you lend him the £10.'

Paddy the Englishman, Paddy the Irishman and Paddy the Scotsman were staying in the world's tallest hotel, some sixty storeys high.

However, the lifts had completely broken down so they had to climb the stairs.

'Let's tell sad stories,' said Paddy the Englishman, 'and that will make climbing the stairs seem shorter.'

So Paddy the Englishman told sad stories for thirty flights of stairs and then Paddy the Scotsman told sad stories for thirty more flights.

Just as they neared the top, Paddy the Irishman said 'I've got the saddest story of all to tell. I've forgotten to collect the key to our room from the desk on the ground floor.'

Paddy the Englishman, Paddy the Irishman and Paddy the Scotsman were out fishing in a boat on a lake together and doing very well.

'This is a terrific spot for fishing,' said Paddy the Englishman. 'How will we know where this spot is next time?'

'I've thought of that,' said Paddy the Scotsman, 'I've just put a mark on the side of the boat.'

'You fool,' said Paddy the Irishman, 'how do you know we will get this boat the next time?'

Paddy the Englishman and Paddy the Scotsman were walking through the woods when they saw a sign reading – TREE FELLERS WANTED

'What a pity Paddy the Irishman isn't with us,' said Paddy the Englishman, 'or we could have got those jobs.'

Paddy the Englishman, Paddy the Irishman and Paddy the Scotsman arrived up at a big hotel only to be told by the manager that there were no rooms available.

'I'm descended from the Kings of England,' said Paddy the Englishman. 'You must have a room for me.'

'Sorry,' said the manager. 'No rooms available.'

'I'm descended from the Kings of Scotland,' said Paddy the Scotsman. 'You must have a room for me.'

'Sorry,' said the manager. 'No rooms available.'

'Look,' said Paddy the Irishman, 'if the Pope arrived up now, would you have a room for him?'

'Well,' said the manager, 'if the Pope arrived, I think we might find a room for him.'

'Great,' said Paddy the Irishman. 'The Pope can't make it – I'll have his room.'

Paddy the Englishman, Paddy the Irishman and Paddy the Scotsman were having a competition to see who was the best magician.

Paddy the Englishman took off his top hat and produced a rabbit from it.

Paddy the Scotsman took a bottle of whiskey and made it disappear.

Paddy the Irishman asked Paddy the Englishman and Paddy the Scotsman each to give him £10 and when they did, he turned into a pub.

Paddy the Englishman, Paddy the Irishman and Paddy the Scotsman owned three big shops side by side with Paddy the Irishman's shop in the middle. One day Paddy the Englishman put up a big sign which said:

MONSTER SALE – HUGE BARGAINS

Not to be outdone, Paddy the Scotsman also put up a sign which said:

MONSTER SALE – HUGE BARGAINS

Soon after, Paddy the Irishman put up a sign on his shop. It read:

MAIN ENTRANCE TO SALES

Paddy the Englishman, Paddy the Irishman and Paddy the Scotsman were being conscripted into the army so they had all their teeth extracted to avoid the draft. Paddy the Englishman was exempted because he had no teeth. Paddy the Scotsman was exempted also because he had no teeth, but Paddy the Irishman was exempted because he had flat feet.

Paddy the Englishman, Paddy the Irishman and Paddy the Scotsman were taking part in a competition to see who was the laziest of the three of them. There was a prize of £100 for the winner.

Paddy the Englishman walked up to the judges and said, 'I'm so lazy I won't even bend down to pick up money I've dropped.'

Paddy the Scotsman walked up to the judges and said, 'I'm so lazy I won't even walk to the bar when I'm offered a free drink.'

Paddy the Irishman lay on the ground where he was and said to the judges in a slow drawl, 'Roll me over and put the prize in my pocket.'

Paddy the Englishman, Paddy the Irishman and Paddy the Scotsman applied for a job on a building site but the foreman was not anxious to employ them.

'Lift this two-ton boulder,' he said to Paddy the Englishman. Paddy the Englishman couldn't so he didn't get the job.

'Empty this thousand gallon tank with a teaspoon,' he said to Paddy the Scotsman. Paddy the Scotsman couldn't, so he didn't get the job either.

'Wheel a barrow of smoke across the site for me,' he said to Paddy the Irishman.

'Certainly,' said Paddy the Irishman, 'just fill it up for me.'

Paddy the Englishman, Paddy the Irishman and Paddy the Scotsman all went to Hell.

Paddy the Englishman wound up in a blazing furnace and Paddy the Scotsman was put in beside him burning away.

Paddy the Irishman wound up in a big bedroom with a beautiful blonde film star in his arms.

'That's not fair,' said Paddy the Englishman and Paddy the Scotsman, 'rewarding him like that.'

'That's not Paddy the Irishman's reward,' said the Devil, 'that's her punishment.'

Paddy the Englishman, Paddy the Irishman and Paddy the Scotsman were captured by cannibals and told that if they could not escape, each of them would be skinned and eaten and their skin turned into a canoe. Each was allowed one weapon to help him escape.

Paddy the Englishman chose a gun but he soon ran out of bullets and was captured. He was skinned, eaten and his skin turned into a canoe.

Paddy the Scotsman chose a knife but he was soon overpowered by the cannibals. He was skinned, eaten and his skin turned into a canoe.

Paddy the Irishman asked for a fork.

'A fork?' they said. 'You won't get very far with that.'

Paddy the Irishman grabbed the fork, pricked himself all over with it and said, 'now try turning my skin into a canoe.'

Paddy the Englishman, Paddy the Irishman and Paddy the Scotsman were invited to have dinner with a bishop. They were told that the bishop was very formal and that everything said at the meal had to be chanted in rhyming verse.

Paddy the Englishman went:
'Your honour divine
Will you pass me the wine?'
Paddy the Scotsman went:
'Your honour supreme

Will you pass me the cream?'
Paddy the Irishman went:
'You baldy headed bugger
Will you pass me the sugar?'

Paddy the Englishman and Paddy the Scotsman were playing golf together when Paddy the Englishman's ball hit Paddy the Irishman. When Paddy the Irishman came to, he said to Paddy the Englishman, 'That will cost you five thousand pounds in compensation.'

'But I said fore,' said Paddy the Englishman. 'I'll take it,' said Paddy the Irishman.

Paddy the Englishman, Paddy the Irishman, Paddy the Scotsman and Paddy the Welshman were in a pub together drinking beer when a fly fell into each of the four glasses.

Paddy the Englishman threw his beer away.

Paddy the Irishman picked out the fly and drank the beer.

Paddy the Welshman threw away his beer but ate the fly.

Paddy the Scotsman drank his beer but sold his fly to Paddy the Welshman.

Paddy the Englishman, Paddy the Irishman and Paddy the Scotsman were all in jail and the ruler of the country was visiting the prison.

'I'm innocent, I'm innocent,' screamed Paddy the Englishman. 'Get me out of here at once.'

'I'm innocent too,' screamed Paddy the Scotsman. 'Get me out of here before I go mad.'

'How about you?' the ruler asked Paddy the

Irishman.

'I'm as guilty as hell,' said Paddy the Irishman. 'I'm entitled to be here.'

'Get this guilty man out of here at once,' said the ruler, 'before he contaminates these innocent men.'

Paddy the Englishman, Paddy the Irishman and Paddy the Scotsman were taking part in a survey about tea-drinking habits.

'I always stir my tea with my left hand,' said Paddy the Englishman.

'I always stir my tea with my right hand,' said Paddy the Scotsman.

'How about you?' Paddy the Irishman was asked.

'Oh me?' said Paddy the Irishman, 'I always use a spoon.'

Paddy the Englishman, Paddy the Irishman and Paddy the Scotsman were all talking about their plans to make a lot of money.

'I'm going to buy a herd of cows,' said Paddy the Englishman, 'milk them morning and night and sell the milk.'

'I'm going to buy a flock of sheep,' said Paddy the Scotsman, 'shear them twice a year and sell the wool.'

'Both your plans involve too much hard work,' said Paddy the Irishman. 'I'm just going to buy a swarm of bees, and every morning at daybreak I'll release them into the park opposite my house. They will visit every flower in the park and make honey while I relax.'

'But the park doesn't open its gates until

nine o'clock,' said Paddy the Englishman.

'I know where there is a hole in the fence,' said Paddy the Irishman.

Paddy the Englishman, Paddy the Irishman and Paddy the Scotsman were hungry one night and had money only for a small pie. Since it was too small to divide they decided to go to sleep and the pie would go to the person who had the most interesting dream.

When they woke up in the morning, Paddy the Englishman said, 'I had a very interesting dream. I dreamed I was ruler over the whole world. You can't get more interesting than that, so I deserve the pie.'

'Hold it,' said Paddy the Scotsman. 'I dreamed I was ruler over the whole universe, so that pie belongs to me.'

'I had the most interesting dream of all,' said Paddy the Irishman. 'I dreamed I was hungry, so I got up and ate the pie.'

Paddy the Englishman, Paddy the Irishman and Paddy the Scotsman were all sentenced to be hanged but were allowed to choose the tree from which the execution would take place.

'I'll choose an English oak tree,' said Paddy the Englishman and he was blasted into eternity.

'I'll choose a Scottish mountain ash,' said Paddy the Scotsman and he went the same way.

'I'll choose an Irish gooseberry bush,' said Paddy the Irishman.

'But that would take twenty years to grow

tall enough,' said his executioner.

'I don't mind waiting,' said Paddy the Irishman.

Paddy the Englishman, Paddy the Irishman and Paddy the Scotsman were boasting about how old their families were.

'I can trace my family back to the War of the Roses,' said Paddy the Englishman.

'My family,' said Paddy the Scotsman, 'had their names on the passenger list with Noah in the Ark.'

'At the time of the Flood and Noah,' said Paddy the Irishman, 'our family had their own boat.'

A rich American challenged Paddy the Englishman, Paddy the Irishman and Paddy the Scotsman to drink ten pints of Guinness in ten minutes.

Paddy the Englishman tried but could manage only five pints.

Paddy the Scotsman did a bit better – he drank seven pints in ten minutes.

Paddy the Irishman downed the ten pints in nine minutes and as the American handed over the prize money he remarked, 'I didn't think you could do it.'

'I knew I could,' said Paddy the Irishman, 'because I did the same thing in the pub next door a few minutes ago.'

Paddy the Englishman had a big dog and Paddy the Irishman and Paddy the Scotsman asked him what breed it was.

'It's a cross between a Scotsman, an Irishman and an ape,' said Paddy the Englishman. '

In that case,' said Paddy the Irishman, 'it's related to all three of us.

Paddy the Englishman, Paddy the Irishman and Paddy the Scotsman were in charge of a branch of a bank in a little country village. One day an inspector from the central office went down to visit them and see how they were getting on. He found the bank closed during banking hours. When he looked in the window, he saw Paddy the Irishman, Paddy the Englishman and Paddy the Scotsman playing poker with the bank's money. Furiously, the inspector activated the alarm bell which rang loudly three times. Nothing happened for a few minutes – then a barman from the pub across the road from the bank arrived up with three pints of porter on a tray.

Paddy the Englishman was giving evidence in court when Paddy the Irishman and Paddy the Scotsman were accused of being drunk and disorderly.

'Tell the court what you saw,' said the judge.

'Well,' said Paddy the Englishman, 'Paddy the Irishman was throwing five pound notes away and Paddy the Scotsman was picking them up and handing them back to him.'

'Thirty days for perjury,' said the judge.

Paddy the Englishman and Paddy the Scotsman were boasting about the size of their estates.

'I can get into my car at seven o'clock in the morning,' said Paddy the Englishman, 'and drive and drive all around my estate and not get back until four o'clock in the afternoon.'

'I can get into my car at six o'clock in the morning,' said Paddy the Scotsman, 'and drive and drive all around my estate and not get back until seven o'clock in the evening.'

'I had an ould car like that too myself once,' said Paddy the Irishman.

Paddy the Englishman, Paddy the Irishman and Paddy the Scotsman were boasting about how famous their uncles were. 'My uncle is a bishop,' said Paddy the Englishman, 'and when he walks down the street, everybody says, "Your Lordship".'

'My uncle is a cardinal,' said Paddy the Scotsman, 'and when he walks down the street everybody says, "Your Eminence".'

'My uncle,' said Paddy the Irishman, 'weighs twenty-seven stone, and when he walks down the street everybody says, "God Almighty".'